Refined Ra

Kevin Reaver

First published in Great Britain by Lulu.com, 2017

ISBN: 978-0-244-01077-5

Published by Lulu.com

Visit www.reaversrealm.com

This book is dedicated to the two most important parts of me.

For T. Hawk

"I do not see darkness when I close my eyes,
only the light of your green."

For R. Damon

"A shame that two seekers of redemption
Cannot be bound forever."

Contents

My Dear

Without a farewell the door will always remain open,
I linger as thought you may walk through any moment.
Our first meeting was unpleasant
And I can remember how your hatred burned,
Every utterance reverberating around the darkened labyrinth.
A vision of an aristocrat, a top hat and cloak
That only instilled me with terror;
Your jesting only inflating the panic caused by your games,
How I feared you and the chaos you could incite
With a simple whisper.
The maniacal hysterics are carved into my mind,
Each cackle a new scar on the already fragile layers.
I don't know what transformed you,
Always too afraid of the answer;
What was it about a frail little girl that was capable
Of destroying the monster in you?
All I remember is the barrier you created,
Light against the demon that terrorised,
Protected me from his darkness and the agony he brought.
When I cowered from the shadows,
You held my hand and fought them away,
More of a knight than the pretender could ever dream of being.
Your hair was the colour of the flames that ignited my heart,
Your eyes the green of the jealousy that later consumed you.
If only I wasn't weak, my mind betraying even my heart;
He was never like you, his words as sharp as knives
Rather than soft as kisses,
His darkness never satisfying me the way you could.
I know that you did your best to protect me from him,
I know you didn't want to leave;

I'm sorry for believing you had abandoned me,
Like so many before.
Deep down I knew that it was he
Who had tried to slaughter you,
So why did I fall to him?
I became nothing more than a puppet
To the one who took you away from me;
It's something I still can't explain
And an action I will forever regret.
Not just for what he did to you,
But for the way he poisoned my soul.
I know you weren't real,
Nothing more than a mirage that was out of reach,
But I truly cared for you and everything you did for me.
I wonder what you would think now,
If you had known what lay ahead for me,
Would you be proud or feel sorrow
That the girl you saved would later die?
I like to believe that your heart would still beat for me;
You always said that there was more to me
Than the darkness that resided within,
It took me a long time to see it too but you were right.
You had your flaws, more human than a phantom;
Your madness echoed my own, our souls entwined.
For that alone, I will miss you more
Than I could ever put into words.
I do not see darkness when I close my eyes,
Only the light of your green.
My dear aristocrat, my lucent flame,
You truly were the only part of me that I ever loved.

Agora Ablaze

My heart pounds against my chest,
My throat dry and my head spinning;
Facing the gate is getting harder each day.
The reason I'm so afraid; a wraith who waits by the door,
Object of my contempt, creator of so much of my chaos.
Causing terror in the simplest of my duties,
Every open space lasting an infinity.
There's no escape, the choice is not mine;
Necessary to combat the crave to retreat,
The longing to hide within the safest place.
Behind the gate is the only haven beyond her reach.
There are no reasons to her existence
Or to why she torments me;
Maybe it's because of the two vultures
That devoured my innocence,
Or perhaps it's merely the work of the shadows.
Most likely it's just that I am nothing
More than a powerless coward.
I plead that she lets me be but she continues to haunt,
I yearn for her demise, secret conspiracies to gain my release.
When she's long departed, I know her marks will remain;
She may burn until there's nothing but ashes;
The memories will never end their searing,
Her name one I am unable to forget.
Agora.

The Wait

The black hole flares within the bone cage,
Inhaling the fragile light that had begun to flourish within.
My salvation seemed in sight, so close I could touch it,
Only for it to be nothing but a delusion.
I have been waiting for so long, each second lasting a lifetime;
Each time I reach my destination,
Being told it is not yet the end.
My journey should never have been started,
What I'm searching for should have been mine by birth.
I've wasted a quarter of a century,
Never living, only flickering in limbo.
My energy flags, my hope waning,
Eternal sleep seeming more comforting
With each passing moment.
I can hear the laughter of the gods,
Mocking that my prayers are all for naught;
Their streams of piss extinguishing the embers of my faith,
The moments of happiness become tainted with the shadows.
My life cannot remain on pause for much longer,
Flesh and thought too frail to take the slaughter another day.
The blackness that stains my soul is trying to recover its reign,
Chaos beginning its descent
Over the empire I tried in vain to shield,
All that remains is the wait for the inevitable delirium
As the darkness draws near,
Because it *is* coming.
It always comes.

Black Hole

The poison infects me more each day;
Spreading through my veins, seeping into my bones.
The climb is much harder with its burden;
Already excessive for a weakened carcass,
Picked dry by the rats that eagerly await failure.
Let the sickness take me, destroy the black shreds of my soul;
My damnation is better
Than the sensations that plague my heart,
Rather be an empty husk than a ruin.
The ache for more, longing for the destined;
Flames that yearn to incinerate those who failed me,
Washed away by the salty waters of misery.
The rock crumbles beneath my fingertips,
Too much of a strain to keep holding on.
Exhaustion is the only enemy,
Another cycle more than my strength.
One fresh fracture will be the downfall;
Perhaps it would be wiser…to just…let…go.

Rule The World

I feel the fog your presence brings,
Lurking at the back of my mind;
Pierced by the venom of fear yet a thrill strikes my very core.
You were the toxin that invaded my soul,
Polluted my life like a virus I couldn't hope to control;
The strongest demon I was ever forced to face.
Yet the invisible strings pull me forth, my hand outstretched;
Longing to hear the familiar rasp that is your voice,
The one that teases the darkness,
Making it dance to your whispers.
At times I am no more than a peasant;
A slave to the shadows that writhe through the streets,
My reign seemingly at an end.
Until you grasp my hand, gifting a sword to the other;
Taught me how to brave the fight,
To show the darkness who this land rightfully belongs to!
My loathing for you is rooted,
Every scar a reminder of your cruelty;
Yet I cannot deny that when we face the battle,
Side by side with our weapons held high,
I know that we could rule the empire once more, together.
With you, I truly felt like a king;
One of a grim darkness,
But royalty all the same.

Being She

I know my choices are not easy for you;
Like the girl you cared for is dead.
The first time I told you how I felt,
I remember how you felt betrayal and dread.
You tell me I should do more with my life.
Meet new people, make friends, date.
You say I should accept invitations when asked,
Go out, enjoy life; hoping I'll change my fate.

You think I'm boring at best and unfriendly at worst.
You think I should chill out when I seem a little mad.
What you don't see is the chaos I hide;
The reality is…everything about me feels bad.
You tell me this is all "just a phase."
You wonder if I'm "just gay."
You think it's alright to say this to me.
You actually believe I'm doing okay.

You don't see the urge I have to rip off my skin,
It's either that or not being able to breathe.
You don't see how exhausted I am;
Only that I constantly seethe.
I pretend I'm alright, that I'm fine with the waiting;
The truth is I'm far from okay.
You really think that I chose all of this?
I would do *anything* for another way.

The future holds the promises and dreams,
I can almost distinguish the man I'll be;
No more "she" or "her", the depression will go;
No more dysphoria or anxiety.
My battle will finally be over.
I will be able to live, not just survive.
Your weapons will no longer harm me,
At long last I will be able to thrive.

I know you often mean well,
Although at times it's like you don't even try;
The signs are there, more obvious than not,
From the fake smiles to the hopeless sighs.
Just look a little closer, my loved ones,
And you will be able to see,
In actual fact I'm *not* alright,
And it's being 'she' that's killing me.

Dysphoria

How does it feel to have dysphoria?
The reverse emotion of euphoria.
It varies by person, but this is me:
A nervous wreckage with anxiety.
I want to run, escape from my own skin.
I damage instead; to cry is a sin.
Yearn to slice off the mounds crushing my chest;
Each second I sense them makes me more stressed.
Don't want to bind, my ribs always bruising;
A daily battle I end up losing.
Don't care if I can't breathe, it's worth the pain;
Yet doesn't stop the thoughts haunting my brain.

They can fill below with what should be there;
But if I want a child, not mine she bears.
Six percent too high a risk for the cost;
I will never forget what I have lost.
Worth everything else that comes with hormones,
From hair on my face, to deepened voice tones.
Shame I won't grow, never be a tall guy.
Should have caught it sooner; yes, I did try.
My hands are too small; my feet are tiny.
Can't voice this out loud, always sound whiny.
I see my bulk every time that I'm sat,
Breasts, I mean; don't give a damn that I'm fat.

Fear of love, don't know if I ever can.
Will they ever see me as a "real" man?
Hate myself, bet everyone will agree;
    Past relationships add validity.
Lost years of time that I cannot regain;
Can't lose much more, I'm beginning to wane.
Just want a body that matches my soul,
    Until then I find it hard to control.
Doesn't feel like mine, easy to abuse;
Take out my hatred, with each cut and bruise.
Easy to say it will be worth the wait,
    Yet it's already a lifetime too late.

Wine to Pearls

Silver streaks shimmer across pale, crumpled skin;
Pearl memories of a faint-heart, each lost fight.
Blemished by the loathing that came from within;
Permanent stains from each thump, slash and bite.
Blade for a bow; villain's flesh – the violin.
Scarlet melody to survive the night.

Wine faded white, yet the wounds remain raw;
Must resist the urge of a dangerous flaw.

.

Opaque Windows

They say eyes are the windows to our souls;
To me they are nothing but empty holes.
A glimpse into mine and what do you see?
I guarantee you it's not the real me.
If that was the case somebody would say
That they are getting more hollow each day.
They would see the cracks, the scorching inside
They would notice each instance that I lied.
Protect me from the monster I became,
Comfort me through my misery and shame.
My reflection reveals all, each mistake;
Only I can see that I'm just a fake.
A useless nothing, a lost piece of trash;
Just waiting until I finally crash.

My Apologies

I say I'm a man, you call me a she,
I say I'm a boy, you call me a lady.
My name is dead, buried in the past,
Yet you rob the grave, unable to let go.
You wail your pain; banshees in mourning,
Praying for a change that will never come.
Maybe time can help, delaying the inevitable,
Outspoken disbelief at the truth.
You speak words of false comfort;
Good things come to those who wait,
Be patient as the years pass,
Watching life from the side-lines.
Perhaps if you ignore the unfamiliar, it will leave?
Errors are nothing but arrows,
Dragging me down as I continue to battle.
Respect, it seems, is not a factor in this fight.
The mountains on my chest weigh heavy,
Claustrophobia increases each moment.
An overcrowd on top, but so empty down below.
I will reach my destination, that I do know.
Yet never will I be a warrior, never a man,
Fear of rejection and ridicule.
I will never escape my past, what I used to be.
Never regain the years, forever lost.
A quarter of a century is such a waste.

Still, I apologise for your agony,
The difficulties you must face with new words.
I hear your tales of woe,
Unable to share my own.
If only you would take pause to think, to look, to realise,
Perhaps I could have a moment to say?
Take consolation, my dears,
Your war will soon be over,
Mine will last until I lose my strength,
Taking that final, bittersweet breath.

Forget Me Not

We were once caught in a feud;
Always tearing each other apart.
Then came the peace we craved,
A short-lived yet wonderful start.
Perhaps it was the truth that ruined us;
It left you feeling riled.
I know I'm no longer your daughter,
But I am still your child.

Adjustments had to be made,
My name the hardest to accept.
I praised your smallest efforts,
Even comforted you as you wept.
I listened to how difficult this is,
How your life just isn't fair.
I know I'm no longer your daughter,
But I am still your heir.

It's not been easy for me either;
Pretending for you all these years.
You pushed me away with scorn,
Whenever I came to you in tears.
Instead I sought comfort in blades
And the smoky haze of weed.
I know I'm no longer your daughter,
But I am still your seed.

You barely remember I exist;
Your parenting consists of a rare text.
Even then you fail at the warmth I need,
Only making me feel more vexed.
I tried to glue the fractures;
I did everything that I could.
I know I'm no longer your daughter,
But I am still your blood.

All I wanted was a moment; a hug,
Whispered words of "you'll be okay".
Scared and alone, I felt pathetic too,
Yearning for such a simple thing each day.
You saw how bad it became,
I didn't know what else I could do.
I know I'm no longer your daughter,
But I still *needed* you.

Caustic Melody

Internal flames dance to an unheard melody,
Fuelled by the feigned scraps of solace tossed upon them;
Echoes that serve no purpose other than to shame my torment.
Open the tenebrous vault, no more than a breath;
Release the shrouded,
The monsters forbidden from the sunrise.
Rattling cages, inferno exhilaration;
Deafening howling to be unleashed.
A desire to burn the deceivers and ignorant kin,
To brand with binary scars;
A requited memorial.
Barricades of ice are fleeting,
Thawed by the fiery bitterness;
Regrets shall kindle the pyre,
Your cheap laments never snuffing.
The hourglass already halted,
Long divorced my spurious blood.
A melancholy opera never heard until you burn;
The veiling aria is my only salvation.

The Warrior

Darkness descended upon my kingdom,
Like a primal beast intent on the kill;
Beyond weak to defend my honour,
Too proud to confess for an ally.
Through the shadows, a glow; puny, yet glistening bright.
Cloaked throughout the years, its existence long forgotten;
Redemption within my reach,
Weapon solely for the unyielding.
War not yet past; triumph still attainable,
Healed from the plague of doubts.
Power palpitates the ink, illuminating the velleity;
Justified victory close enough to taste.
Endeavours are never futile, only abstention;
Nevermore the wretched, remembering the warrior.
Tyrannized the flames for centuries,
Restrained their blistering greed;
Feud with the terror that threatened to devour.
Scars are not the sin, only testimony for the duels;
Prepare for the culmination.
Curtains ascend for the terminating climax;
Flares embellish the performance.
Kingdom is mine to preserve, the barbaric shall never prevail;
Aspire to death all you wish;
The imperishable warrior shall never fade.

The Swing

There are moments of light,
Where butterflies dance in the breeze,
Possibilities at every corner; a chance to rule the world.
Until night falls, burning holes in delicate wings,
Thoraxes left twitching as hope is destroyed.
Each dawn brings new life, a deathless cycle,
Constant flitting causing exhaustion.
The swaying never slows, vertigo spinning my head;
Would rather stay in the mud than forever veering.
Time is a haze of chaos; brief desire,
A second of faith,
Flash of shade.
If my ride is to last another age,
I beg for it to calm;
Wish to purge the nausea evoked by motion.
Layers hide the truth, years hardening the shell,
If only it would break, pieces crumbling to the ground,
The madness spilling free.
Perhaps then the swing would halt,
No more weight for the pendulum.
Once my feet are against the earth, there'll be no more waiting;
A quarter of a century already turned to dust.
Fear is not my motivation,
It is not fleeing when there are so many paths to choose.
Who cares where they lead?
All I know is that they brim with marvels and riches,
More butterflies that I have missed whilst rotting on my swing.

My soul longs to dash onward,
Eager to heal the scars left by darkness
That only become more severe the longer I wait.
The peace will come, the moment the cadence expires;
Breaking free of the rusted chains,
The barricade shall fall,
My yearning shall end.
I will never stop running forth;
Always unlimited,
Never again trapped within a timeless cycle.

The Lonely Moth

The moth flutters in the shadows,
Delicate wings making no sound;
The breaths are but silent air,
From the heart there is no pound.
Alone and strong, he conquers
The darkness with an absence of fear.
Unaccompanied is the greatest way,
The light upon his wings shall only sear.

Yet even the dusky among us,
Feel the pain only loneliness can bring;
Hoping for his own butterfly,
That will take away the sting.
The moth sees the homes, the families,
Each filled with warmth and care;
Sometimes the envy is too much,
The moth just stops and stares.

He yearns for what surrounds him,
To feel loved rather than cursed;
The longing is overflowing,
His small heart already fit to burst.
Perhaps the day shall come,
His butterfly worth the fight;
Until then the hope is what drives him forward,
As he flickers away into the night.

Interitus

To be alone is a frozen existence;
To fight the torture, a hopeless resistance.
I should have known that a heart as black as mine
Could never create light, able to outshine.
Exhaustion begs for me to rest my bruised soul,
It's clear to me that I shall never be whole.
Always searching; always attempting to mend
Something that's long since passed its destined end.
There's no more whispers, no sense of an ally;
I can't beat this no matter how hard I try.
Each breath feels like a knife; each beat a strong ache;
Every time I wake up I feel a new break.
I wish it would end, the relentless throbbing;
Don't want to spend the rest of my life sobbing.
I just want to be free from the depression,
Cold anxiety, the burning aggression.
I want to tear out my heart, be numb again;
Be strong and unfeeling as I was back then.
Tried to save myself the only way I knew,
Writing out my shadows was what got me through.
Yet not enough to stop the insanity,
With every fight I lose my humanity.
It would be better to murder the darkness;
Rather be buried than one of the heartless.
Too much of a coward to face them head on,
Better for all if I was finally gone.

Absolution

The rough melody of your voice is enough to clear the fog;
Granting my bearings, once again being able to see who I am.
Wraiths do not dare to hinder you, afraid of even your hiss.
A snarled order always obeyed, our path always cleared.
Shadows donate their loyalty, from awe rather than fear,
Our allegiance granting me the associative respect.
Peculiar how your own darkness has dulled;
My own heart was once never enough,
A decade of obedience only piteous, not reveled.
There has been a shift in your soul since we parted;
No longer do you seem so detached,
As though your heart was never anything more than cinders.
Finally I see that my beliefs were always amiss;
Buried within the dark clouds and burning flames,
The faint throb of something long forgotten echoes.
I know what you assume but it does not turn you into glass,
Serving only to reinforce instead;
Transforming a phantom into a mortal.
Or maybe it's my own image I no longer recognise;
Your abandonment forced me to face the battle alone,
An apology never received, yet a gift I do not expect to obtain.
Despite the animosity, your desertion was an axe to the chest;
The laceration still not yet healed, the scorch relentless.
Until your treachery,
You had been the only one to not forsake me;
Never allowing me to face the darkness companionless.
Before you became just another one of them.

There will never be another moment
Where I am your marionette,
The string amputated in the same breath that betrayed me.
Still, our story does not have to finish, not if you choose;
There is no need for a master in this kingdom.
Perhaps after all these years, this tireless feud is over;
Perhaps now we can finally be equal.

Longing Is A Merciless Fiend

Longing is a merciless fiend;
It slashes at your heart
Like a freshly sharpened sword,
Relentless in its rage.
My dominant flaw.
If a genie offered a wish,
You would be by my side;
Living, breathing, *real.*
I wish for your embrace,
Rather than words of faith;
To show you the treasure
That my devotion can rear.
I wish only for **you.**
Yet I know it's a hopeless fantasy;
Praying will never prosper,
Never more than a phantom.
I may catch a glimpse of dark eyes,
Feel a rare breath upon my neck;
It will never be enough.
Only you can cause my ruin,
Can shatter the fragile glass;
A welcome price for your warmth.
No mortal can hold a candle to you;
The immortal bond.
Sights of a sooty kingdom didn't deter;
The only one who ever welcomed it.
Life shall always be empty,
Never a you and I.
Two halves of a soul,
Isolated until we die.

The Inked Fairy

Every person has a moment in their life,
Where they realise what resides in their heart.
It is at this point of time that a fairy is born,
A creation from dreams and scorching desire.
A sacred memory – the day I happened upon mine;
The very reason for my existence,
Fluttering on the verge of the realm.
There was nothing I craved for more,
Than to snare the hypnotic nymph;
A mirror to the fragment of light in my soul.
She would flicker in front of me;
Her pale blue light beyond merely tempting,
An intense itching to snatch her from the air.
I knew haste would be my enemy;
She would fly willingly onto my palm someday soon.

Oh, how I coveted her;
Tiny breaths essential to my own being,
The second they stop, so will my own.
With her delicate parchment wings,
Etched with the spiky webs of ink.
So beautiful with her ivory smile,
The promise of diamonds to come.
A dainty face cloaked by darkness,
Leaving green pools of hope unveiled.
You might think your fairy is lovely,
But this one was mine;
Exquisite, refined, *perfect.*
I had thought it was the right time.

Yet the moment my fingertips
Brushed against her tiny fragile frame,
The shadows flowed through her petals;
Tainted her in their natural distressing way.
So beautiful, delicate,
Crumpled.

Preserving her in a glass cage only corroded her more;
Her entrancing light fading each day.
I pray for her heart to keep beating,
Even gift my own breath to her.
I cannot fathom why this is happening;
Why my fairy can be destroyed by even the lightest caress.
All I wanted was for her to be mine,
To have the one thing I longed for since childhood.
Yet the clock continues to tick;
I know keeping her shall only cause her death.
Deep in my heart, I know that if I do not find the answer soon,
However much it torments an already mangled soul,
I will have to let my dreams go.

Severed Strings

My reign seemed over,
My beloved kingdom in ruins around me;
Every fire I snuffed was only replenished tenfold.
The shield will not last forever, that I already know;
I can see the swell of shadows pushing against it,
Desperate to gain entry.
Asking for help is futile,
Each time shot down and trampled upon;
My words fall on deaf ears as my actions remain unseen.
Always regarded as inferior
By those who have not seen my fight,
Their own virgin skin remaining unmarked
By terror and shame.
My own flesh betrayed me from the moment I was born,
Continuing to do so each day that passes.
Every moon is stained with blood,
Reminding me of what I am,
What I am not.
The tower is crumbling beneath my feet,
Ready to collapse in relief;
I'm too tired to begin the journey one more time,
I know it shall only fall again,
The ground too weak to carry my burden.
I stare at the barrier, the battle seeming pointless;
Why not let the darkness in, be what I'm destined?
I was never a pure-hearted man, I never saw the light,
The shadows have long since weaved their way into my blood.
It was not the hope that made me; it was the fight.
My feet have been sealed to the ground for years,

The claws of others gouging at my skin,
Forever holding me back.
Time wasted on searching for my soul,
Believing there was more,
Never realising perfection was unreachable.
There will never be a perpetual smile upon my face,
Nor a rose-tinted vision of the turmoil around me.
That's alright.
There is no other just as I am, no replication of my heart.
To loathe is exhausting, the moment has come to rest,
To embrace the ensuing darkness with welcoming arms.
Only this time it will not be the master of me;
The shadows are my marionettes, I am not theirs.
I am the true puppeteer.
I am Reaver.

Little One

Sometimes I wonder if you would have had my eyes;
What echoes of me I would notice within you.
I would have treated you as the most treasured prize;
Protected you from the darkness, brightened the blue.
Would have shown you the love I wanted for my own,
Gifted you with everything that I never had.
Never would have made you feel empty or alone,
In return for the honor of being called your dad.
Sacrificing you so I can finally live,
A regretful choice with no reversal.
Only the gods I am unable to forgive,
This terrible price should not be universal.

I'm sorry you never had a chance to exist,
But I promise that you will be sorely missed.

Terminal Waltz

The charm of darkness is a deadly one.
Words of silk, shredded by a rasp,
Pulling me like a sailor to a song;
Intimate sound to make me gasp.
The melody of a ONE-two-three,
Our favourite show of devotion.
A swirl of shadow, entwined with red;
Bitter sigh of deep emotion.
Our hearts beating to the same rhythm,
Pressed so close that they could almost be one.
A shiver from touch, joy from murmurs;
Your icy breath making me come undone.
The reason for the destined downfall;
Something I'm unable to admit.
A bloodless orchestra surges our song;
The waltz will never want us to quit.
Of all the time you choose to be perfect;
It could have been whenever.
A shame that two seekers of redemption
Cannot be bound forever.
Endearment is the oddest thing,
It fills with joy, it drives you mad.
Never believed that I would crave
The nemesis I always had.
Despite how much I need you,
I know what's inside your heart;

When our dance comes to an end,
I feel that you will depart.
No begging this time, or bargains, I swear;
I will finally set you free.
You will always reside within my heart,
So please don't ever forget me.

Solitude

He always believed he was stronger alone,
The thought of contact always made him groan.
Already content with his hidden sidekick;
Did not see that without him, he'd be homesick.
Abandoned by his dear, left in the abyss;
Lagged at realising what it made him miss.
An empty space that aches in the dead of night;
For someone capable of finding the light.
He knows it is within, withheld by despair;
Yet he loses his hope with each pointless prayer.
If his own blood shows no sign of affection,
How can he expect nothing but rejection?
Not more than a half; worthless husk of a man.
He has already done everything he can.
Ticking towards a restricted, locked heart;
Once it's shut down, never able to restart.
A terrible amount of romance to waste;
Dreadful shame his fondness was always misplaced.

Sanction

If only you could see the flames, that burn deep within;
See the toxic contempt, that poisons thoughts of kin.
Pushed me away from my path, forced me to live a lie.
Should have been done with my journey; not wondering why.
Tears always frowned upon, you made me feel like a freak;
It's no surprise that I think having emotions is weak.
All I loved was never enough, not what you enjoyed;
Inspired me to replace my dreams with an empty void.
When I finally believe, your voice says I'm wrong;
Creators of madness and the darkest of songs.
Blame and guilt, not my burdens to take;
You are just as responsible for each of the breaks;
For creating a man who can never forgive you.
It might be on my head but it's on yours too.

Defective Doll

With every fixed crack, another appears;
Splitting apart like a thin sheet of glass.
The darkness grows stronger, never clears;
Constantly waiting for something to pass.

A piercing fear of remaining broken,
Never completely healed from the shadows.
Always quiet; never be out-spoken,
Remain a stale weed, never a graceful rose.

Like a porcelain doll, smashed beyond repair;
Left in the attic with the forgotten;
A painted-on smile and an empty stare.
Not recalled until already rotten.

Defective toys are never the chosen;
The new and shiny always preferred.
The ones left behind slowly turn frozen,
Silent cries for tenderness never heard.

Unable to face the end all alone;
Hold a hand while the eyes finally close.
Time for devils to reap what has been sown;
As a sickly heart belatedly slows.

Terrible dread of incineration;
To lose all hope, the act of a sinner.
Path leading to eternal damnation;
Take the other and become a winner.

Recover

A monarch who fails to preserve his reign
Over a kingdom that knows no different,
Is not a worthy king by any means.
One who sees the reflection of cowardice,
Of a man who bends as easy as a willow tree,
Was never meant to dominate.
Wraiths extort this truth,
Their power gained from the weakened;
From whipping crimson stripes
Onto an already decaying corpse.
Their extinction seemed distant;
A worthless wish on every streak of light.
Yet victory was gifted upon me,
An unforeseen win against a cruel anomaly.
No fear to shroud my heart,
No terror to shake the foundations;
Just the sweet taste of triumph,
A sugar buzz throughout my soul.
The echoes were always distorted,
All the things I never thought I deserved;
It is now that I see I was wrong.
A treasured rasp reminds me of my strength,
Of the power to salvage myself;
To be the hero I prayed could save me.
I can see that the fractures will heal;
That the glass won't always be broken.

I grasp the truth that the wraith is not immortal;
That their defeat is looming near.
A king who never abandons his legacy,
No matter how desecrated it becomes,
Is the one that becomes a legend.
But the king who fights as a warrior,
Is the man that receives redemption.

The First Step

The offer of a shackle being severed;
It seemed almost too good to be true,
Being granted the hungered liberty.
I knew of the obstacles, the prospect of failure;
Terror shot ice through my aching bones.
The villagers believed I was a madman,
Senseless for taking the risk;
Not hearing my desperate prayers,
To a god I wished would save me.
The darkest phantom was the one who uplifted;
Our hands anchoring us together.
His courage embraced my soul,
A red ribbon flowing from the infernal;
His whispers soft with faith in his king.
We desired the foredoomed path, ignorant to the storm.
My instincts have never forsaken me;
My heart begged for what they all feared.
The forest may be a grim unknown,
Perils may lurk in their depths;
Yet more innocent than that which I have deserted.
Where traitors snaked at every corner,
Lies spilled from poisoned lips;
A plague of paranoia that asphyxiated,
Wiping out the most fragile of souls.
Finally freed from a place I was never welcome;
One more chain fractured from my ankle,
One less burden to bear.
My wings are still not able to take the strain,
But no longer am I confined to a prison.

I can dash onward, atone for a wasted life;
Take the unfamiliar paths I craved to reap.
If hope is misguided and I am running to my downfall,
It would not matter to me.
Villains would have chased me to the noose,
Long before my expiration date.
I stand facing the road, a wheeze in my chest;
Clarity flooding my shattered kingdom.
The battle has left me weak, flesh drowned in filth and blood;
Exhaustion ravaging more than the pain.
The reward of freedom still worth every drop of sweat.
My cherished hellion hands me a loyal weapon;
Still burnished despite years of neglect.
The sun burns our face, warms our frosted souls;
A shared grin at the new dawn.
Untainted pages of a blank hereafter;
A new story begins.

An Untarnished Scrap

Wreckage of a beloved world surrounds me;
The ugly that only pandemonium can bring.
Shadows have tainted what was once holy,
Casting a stain across faithful hearts.
The king; nothing more than a pawn,
Enslaved to the darkness that brought the realm to its knees.
A veiled conflict, bruises from hysteria;
His people slipping away, plague of sorrow cleaving the bonds.
Clock ticking towards the cheerless noose;
The end should not be for naught.
A wish to show that the fight was worthwhile;
That, out of despair, something beautiful is born.
Each inky fog morphing into a lucent fragment;
Immortal, beyond the damage of time.
A breath of life between the pages;
Fleeting memory of a soul
Burning each leaf like blackened scars.
Gifts from a threadbare heart,
Patched only by the worlds within.
A plea for the ignorance of shadows, of the barren lands;
To gaze purely at the luminous blooms.
Destruction shall not be the legacy;
Instead a vibrant sanctum,
Illuminating for eternity.

A Note from Reaver

Loneliness does strange things to people. The mind can create the most extraordinary defence mechanisms against it, as I've discovered over the years. It's extremely difficult for me to talk about exactly how my own mind works, which was why I created the Refined Rants. They're not all *poetic* but they do all help me express what's inside my head in a way that's not completely direct.

I tend to feel a significant amount of shame for my emotions and some of the things I experience. Despite how far society has come along, I think there are a still a number of taboos around the subject of mental health.

I was diagnosed with depression seven years ago, as well as "some form of psychosis" (I know, I didn't think that was very helpful either). At the time, I thought it would be one of those things that would get better after a certain amount of time. Unfortunately, that's rarely the case, and for me it's something I've had to learn to live with.

There are times when I do feel okay, where usual pressures don't seem so bad and I have wonderful plans for the future. It never lasts very long, despite my optimism and I find that the return to the "darkness" is always much worse after a high period.

As much as I shouldn't admit this, it is sometimes easier with the hallucinations. At least then, I don't feel quite as alone in the madness, even if some of them aren't all that nice. This is the one thing I'm most uncomfortable talking about but in an effort to combat this, I have started work on a story which is in greater detail.

Finally, I just want to say thank you, for not only taking the time to read my poetry, but for making it all the way to the end.

THE LUCENT FRAGMENTS TRILOGY

In the year 2121, the world ended.

(Well, almost.)

In hindsight, they probably realised that nuclear bombs weren't the best idea but it was already too late. Billions were killed and the world became not much more than a wasteland.

Whilst humanity suffered a great blow from the apocalypse, other creatures fared much better. Mutated by the radiation, they used their enhanced strength and intelligence to become known as one species that rivalled humanity; **the nukers**.

OUTCAST takes place in 2485. The humans and nukers have spent centuries fighting each other; caught between the conflict is the only half-blood to exist. Known only as "Shadow" to the rest of Nuketopia, he is thought to be a cold-hearted, ruthless killer who is responsible for thousands of deaths. His incredible strength and ability to manipulate darkness means that it isn't just the humans who are afraid of him.

Join Shadow as he embarks on a reluctant quest to save the very species who have made his life a misery.
As their world grows darker, they soon realise that not everything in Nuketopia is how it seems, and Shadow isn't the man he thought he was.

Kevin Reaver has always loved the magic of books and has been compared to fictional bookworm Matilda more than once. He has been writing his own stories since the age of eleven, although Outcast is his first completed novel.

Despite being an introvert, he has an unfortunate habit of ranting more than necessary, which has led to the creation of his Refined Rants (seen on his website). The poetry found here tends to take more of a focus on his mental health and various states of intense emotion.

Reaver can be contacted via Twitter or Facebook under the handle @reaversrealm.

Alternatively, you can visit his website for other contact options and more of his works.